MW01435360

# SUNDAY SPRINTS

Need some motivation?

Do you work better when someone is holding you accountable?

**Come to SUNDAY SPRINTS.**

I host gently-guided writing sprints on Zoom every Wednesday from 6 to 8 p.m. PST and every Sunday from noon to 2 p.m. PST. (Yes, it's called Sunday Sprints on Wednesdays because... why not?)

Here's how it works: I give a new writing prompt every fifteen minutes. You write. That's it.

All sprinters stay on mute. Alone but not alone, you can draw creative energy from the community of writers on your screen. This is a fun, low-pressure environment—a safe space for you to experiment with your writing. No worries: I will never ask you to share your work.

You decide how to use this distraction-free writing time. Work on that screenplay, novel, short story, play, poem, song. Do some therapeutic journaling. Write letters to loved ones. Do some technical writing. Create a D&D campaign. Finish your homework. Seriously, whatever you need to work on.

Let's get that writing done. Together.

**Join the Sunday Sprints Patreon at:**
www.patreon.com/erikpatterson

**Subscribe to the Sunday Sprints mailing list at:**
www.erikpatterson.org/sundaysprints

Made in United States
Troutdale, OR
04/27/2024

19477104R00126